Tad and Pat

by Emmaline Foster
illustrated by Jason Dove

Practice Decodable 2

Mc Graw Hill Education

Bothell, WA • Chicago, IL • Columbus, OH • New York, NY

MHEonline.com

Send all inquiries to:
McGraw-Hill Education
8787 Orion Place
Columbus, OH 43240

ISBN: 978-0-02-132759-1
MHID: 0-02-132759-9

Printed in China.

9 10 11 12 13 DSS 27 26 25 24 23

Tad at a mat.

Pat, to a hat!

Mad Tad!

Pat at a mat.

Tad, to a hat!

Sad Tad.